T0365869

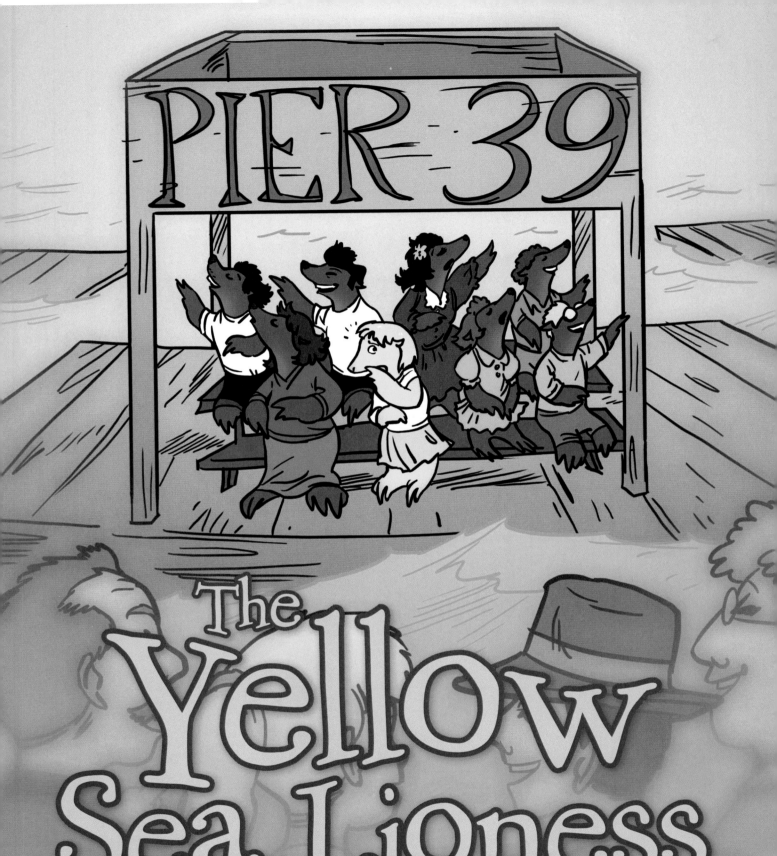

PIER 39

The Yellow Sea Lioness

From the Author of "The Green Tom" and "The Orange Chihuahua,"

KELLY ANN GUGLIETTI

Illustrated by Dwain Esper

DEDICATION PAGE

Dedicated to all of us shy ones. May we have the courage
to explore.

With special thanks to all my chorus and music buddies
and teachers in Binghamton, New York and Hackettstown,
New Jersey for adding the joy of music into my life.

—KAG

AuthorHouse™
1663 Liberty Drive
Bloomington, IN 47403
www.authorhouse.com
Phone: 1-800-839-8640

Published by AuthorHouse 11/03/2014

ISBN: 978-1-4969-4974-5 (sc)
ISBN: 978-1-4969-4975-2 (e)

Library of Congress Control Number: 2014919428

Any people depicted in stock imagery provided by Thinkstock are models, and such images are being used for illustrative purposes only. Certain stock imagery © Thinkstock.

Because of the dynamic nature of the Internet, any web addresses or links contained in this book may have changed since publication and may no longer be valid. The views expressed in this work are solely those of the author and do not necessarily reflect the views of the publisher, and the publisher hereby disclaims any responsibility for them.

authorHOUSE®

The Yellow Sea Lioness

KELLY ANN GUGLIETTI

Illustrated by **Dwain Esper**

Shortly after the Loma Prieta earthquake of 1989, near the Channel Islands off the coast of Santa Barbara, was born a sea lioness, named Lu-sea. As a young sea pup, Lu-sea loved to sing. She had no inhibitions about doing so. She would dress up and sing scales like an opera singer. "Do-re-mi-fa-sol-la-ti-do!"

She would belt out show tunes. "High on a hill was a lonely goatherd. Lay-ee-odl, lay-ee-odl, lay hee hoo!"

She sang gospel. "Oh happy day!" . . . . .

and vintage pop! "Drums keep pounding a rhythm to the brain. La de da de de. La de da de da."

But once in music classes at school, much to the disappointment of Mrs. Soul, her music teacher, Lu-sea froze every time it was time to sing. "From the diaphragm, girls," Mrs. Soul would request. "I cannot hear some of you."

Lu-sea's friend Bubbles would gregariously sing behind her piano at pajama parties, "There's no business like show business!" Lu-sea admired her strength.

Lu-sea would melt at Sandy's soprano solo of "Blue" in concert. "Blue-ue-ue-ue . . . ." Sandy would croon.

Lu-sea laughed hysterically when Croaker and Eddy would do their Sha Na Na impression at Mr. Wittestache's summer music camp in June. "Ar, ar, ar, ar, ar, ar, ar! Sha-na-na-na, sha-na-na-na-na!," they would bark as they shook their shoulders.

Then there was the ever-talented Marilu. Marilu sang operettas with so much power; she did not need a microphone. Her voice rang out to all those who could hear for miles. "L'amour est un oiseau rebelle . . . . ." flowed hauntingly through the sea-torium.

Marilu had a fun, mischievous side as well. After one physical education class, she jumped up on the locker room benches and led the whole class in singing and dancing to the Macarena. Miss. Marm, her P.E. teacher, was not amused.

But Lu-sea grew to deny her enjoyment of singing because she felt her friends sang so much better than she. At the annual field trip in late July to perform on the K-docks at Pier 39, Lu-sea would just clam up. She was sure the tourists were laughing at her when she dared to sing the Bay Area Sea Lion Anthem, "If You're Going to San Francisco." She felt she had no talent whatsoever.

Lu-sea did not realize the talents she did have. All the moms thought
Lu-sea was great at teaching the younger pups the finer lessons in life.

She was the best volleyball player in her region.

Lu-sea always came in first at swim meets . . . .

and could tell jokes that would make even the veteran sea lions roar with laughter.

As Lu-sea entered adulthood, she found her calling as an athletic coach.
Her teaching and athletic skills made Lu-sea a shoe-in for the job.

Lu-sea taught teen pups how to make the meanest serves in volleyball. "Balance the ball on the tip of your nose, girls. Dip your head a little and whack it hard! You can do it!" Lu-sea was often heard to say.

She demonstrated to her swim team the fastest way to propel through the Pacific Ocean. "Just bring those flippers back fast with head forward and off you go!" Lu-sea explained.

Lu-sea's sense of humor and encouragement made her students want to be with her all the more. "You may be only an ion more than a seal as the joke goes, but you are a great world of wonder to me!" Lu-sea exclaimed on numerous huddles before meets.

As Lu-sea grew older, her students surpassed her abilities and won awards of their own. Lu-sea looked on with great admiration and satisfaction. She could not believe she had influenced some of her students to such greatness.

While on a retirement vacation on the K-docks, Lu-sea began to reflect on her life. She was amazed at her accomplishments – so much so that she began to sing out loud!

Heads lifted and bodies rolled in her direction. The other sea lions on the docks began to sing beautiful harmony with her. They clapped their flippers in praise.

Lu-sea mustered the courage to sing at a karaoke night. She told all her friends about the upcoming adventure.

Little did Lu-sea know that her friends arranged for all her students and some of the other sea lions that were so recently taken by her voice to come to her debut. They planned a surprise celebration in her honor after the show. What a sign of appreciation!

The moral of this story is that we all have a unique bundle of talents and interests that we may take for granted. Enjoy the journey in developing them and sharing them with others. You'll be surprised at your influence, being just the way you are.

Dear Parents, Teachers and Guidance Counselors:

I hope you have enjoyed sharing this story with your child(ren) or student(s). You will find four activities on the next few pages that encourage them to think more about the story and respond to it in different ways. Feel free to pick and choose which activities you believe will fit your audience.

Catch my other books, "The Green Tom" and "The Orange Chihuahua." There may be more! Until then, best wishes for a more literate and compassionate tomorrow.

Kelly Ann Guglietti

FUN LITERACY ACTIVITY 1
IDIOMS, IDIOMS, IDIOMS!

Idioms are expressions made up of words or phrases that do not necessarily mean what they say. Make your best guess at the following idioms:

Page 2. Scales —

Page 12. Clam up —

Page 17. Shoe-in —

Page 18. Meanest —

Page 25. Taken –

Can you think of four more idioms? You can ask an adult to help you if this is new. No need to be shy!

1.

2.

3.

4.

FUN LITERACY ACTIVITY 2

Have you ever been shy about doing something? Write about it. Tell:

- What it was you were shy about.
- Why you were so shy.
- If you tried it. Yes or no.
- How it felt to try or not to try it.
- If you would try again or continue to do what made you so shy.
- How you feel now.

_____

_____

_____

_____

_____

_____

_____

_____

_____

_____

_____

_____

FUN LITERACY ACTIVITY 2

Have you ever been shy about doing something? Write about it. (Continued)

_____

_____

_____

_____

_____

_____

_____

_____

_____

_____

_____

_____

_____

_____

FUN LITERACY ACTIVITY 3

Had Lu-sea not been happy enough to sing while on her vacation at the K-docks, would she have discovered that others *did* appreciate her voice? How do you think the story would have ended if she did not sing? Illustrate and write a new ending to this story in one or two sentences below.

FUN LITERACY ACTIVITY 4

BEFORE AND AFTER

Draw a picture of what you looked like when you were afraid to try something. Then draw a picture of what you looked like after you overcame what you were afraid of.

Before	After

Printed in the United States
by Baker & Taylor Publisher Services